HUMAN VALUE
An Ethical Essay

HUMAN VALUE
An Ethical Essay

BY

HENRY STURT, M.A.
QUEEN'S COLLEGE, OXFORD

CAMBRIDGE

AT THE UNIVERSITY PRESS

1923

σοφόν τοι τὸ σαφές, οὐ τὸ μὴ σαφές.

EURIPIDES.

CAMBRIDGE
UNIVERSITY PRESS

University Printing House, Cambridge CB2 8BS, United Kingdom

Cambridge University Press is part of the University of Cambridge.

It furthers the University's mission by disseminating knowledge in the pursuit of education, learning and research at the highest international levels of excellence.

www.cambridge.org
Information on this title: www.cambridge.org/9781107453661

© Cambridge University Press 1923

First published 1923
First paperback edition 2014

A catalogue record for this publication is available from the British Library

ISBN 978-1-107-45366-1 Paperback

PREFACE

THE following essay makes a return to the Greek tradition in its method of studying ethics, the tradition of considering ethical questions in very close connection with politics. The business of the moralist is to explain the nature of virtue and the conditions of the virtuous life. Now the social and political system within which a man lives has an immense influence upon him morally. Plato recognized that. The main lesson of the *Republic* is that a good personal life is possible only in a good state. We cannot say what a good life is unless we have made up our minds what sort of state is good. Englishmen, with their traditional individualism, have tended to overlook this fact The present essay has been written, quite frankly, with certain political pre-judgments.

The last essay of a similar character by a British thinker is Mill's *Utilitarianism*. There too behind arguments on moral questions lie convictions as to the direction which political and social reform ought to take. Mill's principles were those of early-Victorian liberalism; very useful in their day, but not adequate to the problems which confront us now.

The ethical and psychological analyses of the following pages will probably be questioned; they deal with matters about which there have always been great differences of opinion. But, even if his arguments were refuted in detail, this would not shake the writer's faith in his general view that what is right for individuals in their private conduct cannot be settled without reference to what is right for them in their wider relations with their fellow-men.

H. S.

OXFORD, 1923

CONTENTS

CHAPTER I

THE CHIEF PRINCIPLE OF MORALS

§ 1. A man is virtuous who has such qualities that he can live a good life as a member of society. This is not a definition, but a description. It does no more than express the opinion that virtue is an attribute of persons, and that it belongs only to those who live a social life.

Virtue, then, is primarily and directly personal, and exists in the minds of men; but moral quality may also be manifested secondarily by institutions. We can speak of institutions as 'morally good,' if they are so constituted as to increase the welfare of the citizens, and to give opportunity for the exercise of virtue by those who take part in them. Institutions are very powerful in their influence upon the individual. It is not difficult to live virtuously when one's way of life is determined by morally good institutions. This is what social reformers hope from the future; and this is what justifies the zeal with which they labour to change the present state of things. On the other hand, a virtuous life is difficult for any one who is brought closely into contact with and compelled to work under bad institutions; such, for example, as the close oligarchy of Venice, the court of Louis XV of France, or an unreformed city-corporation in eighteenth-century England.

Moralists are not agreed as to what is the chief element in virtue. Most of them hold that virtue is not a simple quality, but is composed of elements. But they are not agreed as to its composition, nor as to the relative importance of the elements. The present essay, without going so far as a complete analysis of virtue, attempts to identify its chief element.

Whatever the chief element in virtue may be, it must be a natural human motive; that is, one which impels men to act, apart from deliberate reflection. If this is not so, we must hold that unreflecting men cannot be virtuous; which seems to me intolerable. We ought not to acquiesce in any ethical theory which denies moral value to the vast majority of mankind.

A natural motive can be transformed into a principle, if it is reflected upon and deliberately approved. For example, unreflecting persons such as children often act benevolently, from mere good-nature. The same persons when grown up may act with equal benevolence, but thoughtfully and approving that line of conduct 'on principle.' The chief element in virtue must be a natural motive which is acted upon by all kinds of men, usually without reflection; but in men of developed intelligence with reflection, as a principle. And this is the chief principle of morals.

The moral principle which is of paramount importance for the individual must be equally important for institutions. If in their moral improvement men show more and more the working of the chief principle of morals, so must the institutions under which they live.

The best-known theories of the chief moral principle which have been put forward are those of Perfection, Moral Law, Reason and Benevolence. None of them seems to me convincing; the best does no more than recognize a subordinate element of moral virtue.

The theory of the present essay is that the chief principle of morals is appreciation of what is good in man. A man is actuated by this motive when he appreciates human characters, acts and institutions as intrinsically valuable, apart from any selfish gain of his own. Sometimes I shall speak of this sort of appreciation as 'human valuation.' For shortness sake I call this moral principle the principle of human value. This is the element which is indispensable to virtue; there are other elements in virtue, but without this one a man cannot be virtuous. It manifests itself also in institutions; and the presence of that element in them is the chief reason why we call institutions morally good.

A few examples will show how I think that

human minds manifest human valuation: a boy who admires the powers of some boyish leader; the same boy a few years older who reveres his mother as a pattern of all the gentler virtues; a man who, reading the story of the last days of Socrates, does homage to the law-abiding spirit which made him refuse to escape from custody; a man who appreciates his native state as an excellent political institution, in the spirit in which Pericles spoke of Athens in his Funeral Speech; an Englishman who admires the genius and charm of the French nation, though he does not wish to be anything himself but an Englishman. If these admirations or valuations are sincere, they manifest themselves in action. Such acts may be done without reflection; but, when they are done with full consciousness and approval of the motive prompting them, they are done on principle; and then they exemplify the chief principle of morals.

Before proceeding I must consider briefly a preliminary difficulty. Surely not all elements of human nature are excellent or valuable. How do we know, then, what elements are good and what are not? There is in mankind, for example, a strain of cruelty; not present in all men, but certainly in a great number, as we see from the prevalence of teasing in children. Why do we disapprove of it? The question is evidently a very big one. I will deal with it only so far as my immediate purposes require.

As a matter of practice men rely mainly upon the moral standard of the society to which they belong, in deciding what personal qualities are valuable. Human communities work out moral standards suitable to their circumstances, as they work out standards of justice or of politeness. As circumstances vary at different times and in different places, we must not be surprised if standards disagree. But, in regard to any given standard, we may feel pretty sure that it tends upon the whole to promote the welfare of the society which has fashioned it. The main elements of human welfare are well known, though perhaps indefinable; they are physical health and strength, good understanding, artistic excellence and, most of all, moral excellence, which, as I hold, consists mainly in human valuation. Here, some one may object, is a logical circle; an agent is morally good when he appreciates human excellence, and human excellence consists largely in moral goodness. But it will be found that we always commit a logical circle when we try to explain the nature of an ultimate quality: the circle would appear just as much, if we tried to define health, or intelligence, or consciousness itself.

But, though persons rely for moral guidance mainly upon the current standard, they have also an individual power of criticism. In a country where the people are of limited intelligence and economic conditions are stationary, there is very little criticism; simple people conform to their moral standard without reflection, just as they speak their native language. But, in countries which have become progressive,

men criticize. Their criterion is always conduciveness to human welfare, usually the welfare
of the society to which they belong. When a
certain level of culture has been reached, acute
minds see how more welfare may be attained
by developing the principles of conduct which
have already been found to be successful.

And now for a word on method. How is my
theory to be proved? It cannot be proved. It
can only be supported; and this must be done
by appeals to experience. A theory about morals
is primarily psychological. It must give an account of processes which go on in the minds
of persons. One who advocates such a theory
as this of human value, must hold that his own
moral consciousness works in this way and that
the generality of men are like him. In order to
support his theory he must review classes of
facts; he must show, for example, that by the
help of the theory we can understand social and
political institutions in their relation to morality;
and that we can understand the qualities of

character which are called the virtues, and the order of their appearance in society. The establishment of any philosophical theory must be a work of time. It must lie for a considerable season before the world; many men must consider it, and try to understand their experience by the help of it. If the theory gives men more help than any of its rivals, it may be regarded as established; though, of course, it may always be superseded later on by some other theory which is still more illuminating. Any one who demands a short and simple way of proving philosophical theories, does not understand what is possible or desirable in such a case.

Any dialectical proof of an ethical principle can serve merely for purposes of occasional discussion. If a proof of the principle of human value were attempted, it might, perhaps, run somewhat as follows. All agree that Socrates was a good man, and that one admirable feature in him was his law-abidingness. Now why is this quality admirable? Because it conduces to preserve the state. Why preserve the state? Because the state is necessary to the welfare of the citizens. Why consider the welfare of one's fellow-citizens, or of any other set of men? Because there is something excellent in them which entitles them to claim our consideration and service. And so we might argue about the other virtues, the primitive virtues of the tribe and the domestic virtues of a later stage. They all tend towards the development of human bodies and minds. Now, if it is morally good that men should be developed, there must be something in them which is intrinsically worth developing. If men have, as the thorough-going pessimist affirms, no more value than swine, there is no merit in working for them; except with a view to some ulterior purpose. And, for man, there cannot be anything ulterior to mankind.

If human valuation is the chief element of virtue, we can give a formula of moral progress both for individuals and for societies. Moral progress must always consist in a greater prevalence of the chief moral element, whatever it may be: if it is Reason, moral progress consists in men becoming more reasonable; if it is Benevolence, in their becoming more benevolent. I hold that an individual has progressed in virtue when his appreciation of human excellence is strong and wide. He progresses as far as possible when he appreciates all the good elements of human nature which can appeal to him, with all the force of which he is capable. A society progresses morally when it includes an increasingly large proportion of persons who manifest the sentiment of human valuation in an increasingly stronger and wider form, and when its institutions tend increasingly to encouragement of the sentiment.

The chief element of the moral ideal is a catholic appreciation of man. We are short of the ideal so long as there are good elements in man to which we are insensitive. There is nothing static about this ideal. Mankind is always developing new elements of value. The world changes, and the expansion of discovery enables men to come into contact with new elements of the world; so men develop new qualities, and many of the new qualities are admirable. We need not be afraid of realizing the ideal and so exhausting its inspiration; we cannot get to know all the good elements of human nature, even with the longest life of action and study.

We can also give a formula of moral discovery. Men open up new possibilities of virtue when they take new elements of human nature into the range of their appreciation. I think that we can observe such moral changes most plainly in comparing literatures of widely separated epochs. Consider for example a moral standard such as is displayed to us in the Homeric poems. In Homer the qualities which are appreciated are mainly those which are appropriate to warriors and leaders of warlike tribes. Any typical piece of modern literature, *David Copperfield* for example, will show that, though the epic virtues are still greatly admired, other virtues now find

PRINCIPLE OF MORALS   13

a place in modern standards, of which primitive men took but little heed. The moral distance between those far-off times and ours is the result of many moral discoveries. When the appropriate time arrives, men of insight and enthusiasm direct attention to neglected elements of human nature, and introduce new virtues into the current moral standard. Some of these discoverers have been leaders of religion, others philosophers and men of literature.

§ 2. Any one who at this time in the world's history puts forward a new ethical theory must meet a formidable objection: If there is any truth in your theory, why was it not suggested long ago? Briefly, my answer is that the world was not yet ready for it. Such a theory as that of human valuation could have no chance of acceptance, except under social and political conditions which are only beginning to come into existence.

This is just one example of the great influence of institutions upon moral practice and theory.

It is impossible to act upon the principle of human valuation in an unfavourable social environment. And moralists do not put forward theories to which no practice can correspond. Nor is it desirable. Theories out of due season are not worth much; there are appropriate times for inventions in speculation, as there are for inventions in the mechanical arts. But, really, philosophers do not often make the mistake of premature discovery. Like other men they are creatures of limited vision; they cannot see principles which are far below the practical horizon. They do all that can reasonably be expected of them, if they are able to discern the principles which are just beginning to be adopted by the men who are actively engaged in the business of the world.

There is no need to review all the conditions which are necessary for the practical and speculative recognition of the principle of human value. Some of the conditions are religious; and these I wish to pass over in silence, confining

myself to secular matters. One indispensable
condition is that there should exist a widely-
inclusive and solidly established political system;
in other words, a civilized state. This excludes
all primitive or savage conditions of society. The
principle of human value means recognition of
the value of man as man; an Englishman, who
professes it, must admire good human qualities
wherever he may happen to find them. Now
such a breadth of mind is impossible for primitive men, owing to an instinct which I would
call Tribal Antagonism. Men of adjacent tribes,
who live under primitive conditions and are not
included in one political system, naturally hate
each other and cannot recognize each other's
good qualities.

Tribal antagonism is always rife among primitive men. Within the narrow circle of a savage
community there is much good-will and com-
radeship. Savages also have a wonderful power
of sympathy; by which I mean ability to understand each other without overt communication.

But their attitude to strangers is very different. They make hardly any distinction between stranger and enemy.

The strength and antiquity of tribal antagonism may be illustrated from observation of some other gregarious creatures, dogs for example. One of the best-known canine tendencies is that of fighting at sight with a stranger. This has no utility for dogs in their present state of domestication, and must therefore be inherited from the remote past. Naturalists tell us that packs of wild dogs have the habit of keeping each to its own hunting ground and preserving its boundaries jealously against poachers. In Constantinople, in old days when the city was scavenged by pariah dogs, each pack kept carefully to its own quarter, and an intruding dog was instantly torn to pieces.

Such a fact helps us to understand the hatred which prevails between tribes of hunting savages. Curr, writing about the Australian natives, says: "Strangers invariably look on each other as deadly enemies. Before the whites interfered with native manners, no black ever neglected to assassinate a stranger at the earliest moment that he could do so without risk to himself*." There is indeed very little to bring adjacent hunting tribes together, and many causes to provoke hostility. If a stranger is found upon alien territory, the presumption is that he is a poacher.

Like almost every element of our nature, tribal antagonism has its good side; in the remote past it was absolutely necessary to enable tribes to protect their hunting grounds and secure their food-supply. Much as we may deplore the savageries which hunting tribes practise upon each other, we must remember that with them poaching is a matter of life and death. In modern society this primeval instinct may be utilized to stimulate competition, as when a large school is divided into 'dormitories' which play against one another at cricket; and it is an important

* *Australian Race*, i. 64 *et saep. al.*

element in all the athletic competitions which exercise such a wholesome influence upon the lives of young Englishmen. But these playful rivalries are very different from primitive tribal hatred. It is always easy in Anglo-Saxon sport to make up a single team out of two teams which, a little earlier, were contending keenly against each other; as when Oxford and Cambridge agree to row against Harvard and Yale. Antagonism between the parts of a nation should always be kept to the plane of make-believe. If it is serious, it is fatal to good-will and prevents the citizens from appreciating each other.

In civilized societies what keeps tribal antagonism in subjection is the need of co-operation; men must cease from hating when they need each other's help. Civilization is possible only so far as men agree to a division of labour, and share according to some sort of plan the goods which they produce and the services which they perform. The primary and most important kind of co-operation in which men engage over wide extents of country is that of government and, in connection with government, the work of national defence. Nothing brings men together so closely as participation in dangerous enterprises, especially those of warfare. By co-operating in government, in war and also in the large-scale industry which government alone makes possible, men come to understand each other, and recognize each other's merits. This seems to be the fundamental reason why the institution of the nation-state is necessary now, and will remain necessary in the future. Some idealists have advocated that our present big nation-states should be broken up into small city-states; on the ground, I suppose, that political life in such narrow communities is intense, and their spiritual activities very vivid, as in the city-states of ancient Greece and medieval Italy. But, if this were done, tribalism would break out anew. The Greek and Italian city-states were always squabbling and fighting savage little wars; and we should see the old

2–2

animosities revived, if we went back to the old political system.

We do not need in modern society the degree of sympathy which we find among some primitive tribes. By 'sympathy' I do not mean 'pity,' of course, but the power of entering directly into the thoughts and feelings of one's neighbours. Some savages possess it to an extraordinary degree. In Melanesia, for example, the natives are so much in sympathy that they do not need appointed leaders in war or explicit votes when they take decisions in their palaver-meetings*. So close a unity of the individual with his society would probably be injurious to us. But we do need, diffused throughout the wide extent of our nation-states, enough sympathy to neutralize tribal antagonism, to enable nationals to co-operate in national tasks, and so to understand and appreciate each other. And this is the chief moral purpose for which the machinery of the state exists.

* Rivers, *Instinct and the Unconscious*, p. 95.

§ 3. It is not enough merely to establish a state; hearty good-will must also prevail among the citizens, if the prevailing morality is to be of a high type. A state makes good-will possible; but most states are subject to some condition or other which impairs it. The fact is that, even after the cruder manifestations of tribal antagonism have been suppressed, the old instinct is liable to show itself in new forms; men are always ready to take opportunities of hating each other. In India the curse of the country is caste, which puts classes of the citizens into relations of mutual repulsion, so that they cannot co-operate heartily for any purpose; in other countries there are prejudices of colour, as in the south of the United States; elsewhere there are religious hatreds, as in Ireland. In France before the Revolution the citizens were divided sharply into privileged and unprivileged, a division which caused deep irritation, and explains most of the excesses of the Terrors.

Where any one of these causes of internecine

hostility predominates, it is impossible for the citizens to work together heartily, or to appreciate each other's good qualities as men. What chance can the doctrine of human value have in a caste-country, where an upper-caste man regards his lower-caste neighbours as sources of pollution, and will not eat with them, or willingly receive any act of neighbourly kindness from them? Or what chance has it in a country torn by religious hatreds, where one party of the citizens is always blaspheming the religion of the others, and parading the coarsest and most violent contempt for institutions which the others hold sacred? What use would it be to talk of human value to an American cotton-planter; to one, at least, who holds the usual southern prejudices about negro blood? Or to a French marquis of the court of Louis XV, who had not learnt anything from Rousseau?

§ 4. Nor indeed are the prospects of the doctrine favourable wherever there is great unfairness in the distribution of wealth. The trouble arises in relation to capital. Salaries are necessarily unequal, because the services rendered are so different in value; but there is nothing necessary or natural in the existing distribution of capital. Capital, of course, is the accumulated wealth of a society. Many have a large share of it who misuse or waste it; while others, who could use it well, can get no share.

Hence much bitterness. In Russia, where there was extreme class-antagonism under Tsarism, the Great War occasioned an uprising of the proletariat by which the whole capitalist class was swept away. In Germany, where the opposition between propertied and non-propertied, though less than in Russia is still very strong, there is Karl Marx's doctrine of the class-war, which has much vogue among the restless, vaguely discontented people who form the political parties of the extreme Left. Most Englishmen disapprove of class-war and prefer to seek peaceful remedies for admitted social evils. But many intelligent British workmen feel bitterly about the existing distribution of property; sometimes we may hear them abuse employers as 'blood-suckers,' and landlords as 'land-thieves.' And they are sceptical about any sort of virtue or superiority in the upper classes.

The rich on their side requite these sentiments with contempt and dislike. Many secondary differences have developed to increase the separation of classes; differences of manner, speech, thought, taste and general way of life which obscure our common humanity and preclude the sympathy which should unite fellow-citizens. The duke is hardly able to imagine how the docker lives; he is tempted to fancy that he himself is composed of altogether different clay, and that dockers and the like exist solely for his convenience. Under such conditions it would be useless to put forward the doctrine of human value, if there were not a large and increasing number of persons who dislike the existing economic condition of our country, and exert themselves to change it as opportunities present themselves. They realize that in a society where rich and poor hate each other, the social life is weakened and impoverished on every side, most of all perhaps in its morals.

§ 5. Nor is the principle of human value likely to be accepted in any country where the general spirit of the government is out of agreement with it. Systems of government exercise almost as much influence upon thought as systems of religion. Even if the principles which are implicit in a system of government are not clearly avowed or understood, they impose themselves silently on men's minds. And in every society there is a governing class which is attached to the system that it administers by the strong ties of self-interest and the strong prejudices of early training. This class is always the chief arbiter of ideas; no theory of any kind has much chance in a country where the social leaders are solidly against it. Now, up till recent years, the spirit animating governments all over the world has been decidedly against the principle of human value, and even at this day is only beginning to change.

The only kind of government which is decidedly favourable to the principle of human value is democracy; one which is genuinely democratic in practice, and not merely in name. Speaking broadly, we may divide systems of government into two classes, the authoritative and the democratic. In the former the sovereign power rests with some person, or, more usually, with some limited class of persons; in the latter it rests with the mass of the people. The actual business of governing must always be in the hands of men who are specially qualified to govern, but in a democracy the demos controls the governors and puts them into the position of public servants.

Authoritative forms of government are unfavourable to the principle of human valuation, because the governing class despises the masses, and thinks but little of man as man. This is very natural. The populations which live under irresponsible authority are poor and ignorant; they are sunk in low, material cares and have but little consciousness of the state. They cannot make themselves respected by their governors.

Our British government is ceasing to be authoritative, but the traditions and prejudices of the old system are still in vigour among us. States, of course, were not democratic, but authoritative, in their origin. They were not founded by intelligent individuals assembling together and binding themselves by political contracts, as Hobbes and similar theorists professed to believe. Still less were they founded by philanthropists for the good of mankind. The founders of states were ambitious chiefs, who aspired to a wider sphere of authority than chieftainship afforded them, and therefore conquered their neighbours in the style of our Anglo-Saxon kings. Such monarchs are not wide in their appreciations of men, as a rule; nor are their courtiers. The early kings of England after the Norman Conquest gathered round them a band of administrators, counsellors and warriors who formed a governing class, the descendants and successors of which rule us to this day and preserve many of the traditions of monarchical society. Our governing class is always being reinforced by men who have made fortunes in business and desire to rise in the social scale by taking up politics. This has been going on ever since England became a commercial and industrial country. And so the pride and prejudices of wealth become added to those of political position.

Whenever government is in the hands of a class, the general arrangements of the state are sure to favour the members of the class, and those who set the national tone will show special appreciation of the distinctive qualities of the class. If the governing class is such as it was in mediaeval England, the qualities most admired are those of the knight and the courtier; while those of the 'villein' and the 'ceorl' will be despised. Traditions linger after the causes which produced them have disappeared; and so the current appreciations of our society are even more partial than is warranted by our social and political conditions.

The spirit of a democratic government is not narrow in this sense. The general arrangements of the democratic commonwealth are directed towards the welfare of the mass of the population. The personal qualities which are most generally appreciated are the virtues which enable citizens to lead the life of ordinary citizenship; other qualities, such as those of chivalry, will be admired; but in their due place and degree.

There are countries in Europe where democratic principles are recognized formally, and where political machinery exists which might be used for democratic purposes; but where no real democratic system is possible, because of the poverty of the population, and because of the general want of political interest and capacity which is due to poverty. People who are struggling incessantly to keep alive can have no thought for politics. In most of the so-called democracies of the present day, the masses are despised by the governing class, and their good qualities and potentialities are not properly appreciated. So far we have had in Europe no example of a nation-state in which democratic principles are brought into full operation and where the governing class is controlled in the interests of the majority. Our own country cannot yet be so described; the influence of authoritative traditions is still too strong, and there is still too much poverty and ignorance.

What we may hope to see established in our country is a carefully thought-out system of democratic political machinery (which in great part already exists), with democratic institutions, a democratically-minded governing class, and arrangements to ensure an equitable distribution of wealth—the whole vivified by a keen political interest, and purified by a high sense of political duty. All this means earnest thought and careful organization; in the complex conditions of modern society we cannot have these advantages upon easier terms. I do not know that there is current in England any well-recognized term for such a political community. I would suggest that we might borrow the term Social Democracy.

British political development is evidently moving towards social democracy. The masses are beginning to acquire enough power of reasoning and imagination to enable them to study political problems and to control the governing class. New institutions are being set up to benefit the masses, and old institutions are being transformed. Most important of all, the governing class is being changed. Already there are many persons in local government, in the national civil service and in general politics who are inspired by social-democratic ideas, and work with enthusiasm as public servants for the public good. And there is now an important political party which, more or less conscious of the direction of its movement, is working towards the realization of a social-democratic system. When a social-democratic system is established, government will be pervaded by the spirit of catholic human valuation.

§ 6. It will help my explanation of the principle of human value if I criticize some rival theories.

Perfectionism is that with which I disagree least; it assumes that the chief element in virtue is desire to attain human perfection oneself and to see it realized in others; and this has some resemblance to appreciation of human excellence. But the difference between the two theories is not inconsiderable. It seems to me that perfectionism is less true psychologically, and also has some practical disadvantages.

If perfectionism means, as it ought to mean, that men have a definite idea of human perfection which they strive to realize, there is the obvious objection that none but men of reflection can have such an idea. Desire of perfection is not a natural human motive. Children and savages would utterly fail to understand it; they would merely be puzzled if they were told that they were aiming or ought to aim at perfecting human nature. On the other hand, the simplest man can appreciate a fine human character. One who knows a good man when he sees him never needs to think about perfection. The savage perceives some good quality in his leader and admires him for it. A later generation is able to appreciate other good qualities, which do not appear in savage life at all. Men admire what they see or they can imagine; we should be impoverished indeed, if we could not admire anything without reference to perfection.

A great practical objection to perfectionism is that it conduces to excessive conservatism in morals. It assumes that perfection is fixed and finished for ever; the perfect man is a model set up which we have only to imitate. But a static ideal tends to check progress. Moral teachers should beware of claiming finality; we can see obvious faults in the ideals of the past. Even at the present day one may doubt vehemently whether man is anywhere near perfection, or whether any one can frame a moral ideal which will defy the criticism of future generations.

Perfectionism lends itself easily to systems of authoritative teaching. The moral authority— the church or whatever else it may be—knows the perfect man and can give us infallible directions how to make ourselves like him. There are, certainly, some great advantages in having a powerful organization to form ideals and to impress them upon a nation; but they are preponderant only in early stages of society. In a more advanced society they are outweighed by the disadvantage of rigidity.

The spirit of democracy is very different. A democratic society is flexible and adaptable in everything. Its ideals spring from the general consciousness of the community, and they are modified by free criticism. And when society has reached a certain stage of development the moral views of the masses are wholesomer and more trustworthy than those of any limited class.

The Principle of Moral Law has this advantage over perfectionism that obedience to law is natural to man. Our social way of life has implanted in us an instinct of obedience to social rules. This is part of the general deference to constituted authority which men naturally feel. In advanced societies men criticize established laws and moral rules; but a reverential feeling towards them always remains and ought to remain a powerful motive.

The most influential advocate of the principle of moral law is Kant. In his doctrine there is much that is peculiar to him alone, and therefore I forbear to mention many of the objections which have been brought against Kantianism. But there are some objections which hold good against any self-consistent formulation of the principle.

Any one who adheres unflinchingly to the

principle of moral law must be very rigid and hard-hearted. Presently I shall have to criticize the principle of benevolence, and draw attention to its inadequacies; but no moral system can commend itself to the modern world which does not contain a large element of benevolence. The Kantian moralist, however, must be deaf to all the appeals of benevolent feeling. He can make no sort of exception or reservation. The moral law does not exist to increase welfare, it has no reference whatever to welfare or happiness; it must be revered for its own sake. Therefore Kant would treat as merely irrelevant an argument that over-strict enforcement of moral rules must cause unhappiness.

The moral law as thus understood is incapable of change. According to Kant the laws of mathematics are not more unalterable than those of morals. Rules which have reference to welfare can, of course, be modified; conditions of welfare change, following the changes in man and in his environment. But all that is a different story.

There can therefore be no room for criticism of moral laws; nor can any progress or discovery be made in morality.

The moral-law doctrine evidently lends itself readily to systems of authority. Every system of authority has its code of rules which it desires to fix as firmly as possible upon the consciences of its subjects. Persons in authority are always tempted to identify their own particular system of conduct with the absolute moral law.

For those who hesitate to make this identification, but yet hold fast to the principle of moral law in the Kantian sense, there arises great difficulty in saying what the moral law is, and what detailed precepts are enjoined by it. Usually it all results in the consecration of conventional moral rules, as we see from Kant's example. The inner history of Kant's ethics is as follows. He was reared in a very strict pietistic form of Christianity. After he grew up, he lost faith in the dogmas of Christianity, but adhered firmly to its moral rules. As a philosopher he cast about for a theoretical justification of the rules; and the result was his doctrine of moral law.

The principle of moral law has enjoyed a great vogue; but now, like all other kinds of authoritative doctrine, it is less in favour. In democratic societies there is great respect for law both moral and otherwise, but not an undiscriminating respect. Thoughtful men take into consideration the content of a law, or at least the character of those who are the authors of it. Many of our recent laws are too technical for the layman to give a judgment on them; but we have confidence in the law-making authority. In regard to ordinary laws we consider whether they conduce to public welfare; and, if not, agitate to get them changed. So with the current system of moral rules; such reverence as we give to it depends ultimately upon our judgment as to its conduciveness to public welfare. We reverence the moral law for the sake of man, not for its own sake.

The Principles of Reason and of Benevolence are also natural motives of conduct. In the writings of the best exponents the principle of reason means love of knowledge; while benevolence-ethics rests upon the kindly feeling of man for man. Even among low-grade savages there is much benevolence in the behaviour of tribesmen towards each other. Love of knowledge appears at a much later stage, but is genuinely natural to some minds.

Plato is the greatest advocate of the principle of reason; both he and Aristotle were full of intellectual enthusiasm. They lived in the bright morning of science, when ardent souls were tempted to think that perfect happiness lay in devotion to intellectual pursuits, and that all moral faults would be cured if men submitted themselves without reserve to the guidance of reason.

But no one in harmony with the modern spirit will agree with Plato. If there is any truth in current psychology, the main impelling motives of human nature are non-rational. Intellectual enthusiasm certainly counts for much with men of exceptional gifts, but not with the majority. And, even with gifted men, intellectual enthusiasm can be overdone. It is possible to live, as Renan said, entirely 'with one's head'; but it is not a satisfactory way of life, because it tends to alienate a man from the mass of his fellow-citizens and to damp the fires of his nature. Nor is reason good as a political principle. The general tendency of those who have adopted the principle is to be exclusive and anti-popular. Plato is thoroughly aristocratic, though his prejudices were not the common ones of wealth and birth. Aristotle's ideal State was a cultured little community, something like Weimar in Goethe's time, existing for the sake of a few intellectuals. But a one-sided devotion to intellectual pursuits is not good, even for the intellectual powers. When men stifle within their breasts the common passions of humanity, they cease to have anything adequate to think

about, or any adequate motives to go on thinking.
Nor is a little, self-contained, cultured state like
Weimar an environment in which the arts and
sciences remain at their best. Great minds are
produced and thrive under a generally vigorous
condition of national life. A nation's energies
slacken, if the interests of the many are subordinated to those of the few, whoever the few
may be.

The Principle of Benevolence can never be
mentioned without deep respect. It has done
splendid service in the past, especially in the
hands of the Utilitarians, whose record is one
of the chief glories in the spiritual history of
our country. I think it has owed much of its
acceptance to the fact that it implies a protest
against the hardness and coldness of other
systems, which insist that we should submit
unconditionally to authority or treat men as
passionless thinkers. At any rate it is a very
human principle.

The principle is right in recognizing that high

virtue is possible only to those who are well-disposed towards their fellow-men. Benevolence is the negation of tribal hatred, class-prejudice and personal bitterness. Such evil sentiments pervert a man's judgment. Only the man who is kindly and sympathetic is in a position to make a proper valuation of man.

But benevolence needs much qualification, both as a principle of personal conduct and as a principle of politics. We ought not in our behaviour to others to allow ourselves to be influenced by benevolence without respect of character. Yahoos have no claim upon us. Mere benevolence is too soft, too undiscriminating. Moreover, it is too commonplace, too humble. By such a principle we may justify the simple duties of everyday neighbourhood; but not the higher flights—the heroisms, devotions and secret aspirations of the moral life.

The general character of the institutions of a good commonwealth should be benevolent; but there must be many qualifications. A community in which there is no hardness must deteriorate in respect of every virtue and every excellence. A certain percentage of human beings are born defective, either in physique, or in morals, or in intellect; if they are not firmly treated, they will drag the community downwards. Society will be like an ill-kept garden in which the weeds have multiplied and choked the good plants. It is a mistake to think that the communities of the future will be in all respects milder than those of the present; in some respects they will be stricter. Governments which are not fully democratic are weak for most purposes, because they do not enjoy the confidence of the people; and are lax, because they are indifferent to public welfare. Weakness and laxity are easily confused with good-nature, and often seek the shelter of the name. The governments of the future will not hesitate to act sternly, if the welfare of the community so demands.

These criticisms upon rival principles of

morality do not profess to be refutations of them, but only indicate some of their weak points. Doctrines of moral philosophy cannot really be proved or disproved by trains of argument. The thinker can only put them forward, and leave the world to judge how far they agree with experience.

The chapters which follow will attempt to support the principle of human value by reviewing some sides of experience. I shall endeavour to show that the principle enables us to understand how organized societies improve in morality, and what the normal order of moral development is in the race. A subordinate principle of morals, which is different in its origin from the chief principle, will be seen on examination to be closely related to it.

If my analyses of moral experience are correctly made, they ought to give some hints for the practical management of life.

CHAPTER II

THE PRINCIPLE IN INSTITUTIONS

§ 1. Societies improve in morality in proportion as their institutions are conducive to appreciation of human value. This may occur in two ways; institutions may be directly moral, or they may conduce to morality by setting up conditions which are favourable to it. In the latter case a trading institution, for example, may arise from motives and be carried on for purposes which are morally neutral; but it may conduce to morality by bringing men together. In the former case an institution such as a custom or a law may be directly moral, because it embodies the principle of human value. I will speak first about the institutions which have indirect moral importance; they form, as it were, the supporting framework of our spiritual life.

Any institution conduces to good morality if it brings men into healthy co-operation, so that they are useful to each other and get to know each other. The most important of such institutions is government. Men who take an interest in the government under which they live are united by something more than external constraint; they are drawn together by co-operation. In early days this was how tribal antipathies were overcome. The king set the example; he looked out for trusty warriors and able officials, and did not care from what part of his dominions they came. And as the size of kingdoms increased, wider circles of people were drawn together. A united England was more favourable to virtue than a Heptarchy.

There comes a time, of course, when expansion does more harm than good. There was no utility in the vast empire of our early Plantagenets, stretching over a great part of France as well as England. It could not, for reasons of geography and language, be unified enough for the people to have common interests and common feeling.

Another great combining influence is trade. Tribes of hunters can do no business with each other; they produce no manufactures, and have no means of storing commodities. But, when men come to have settled habitations and begin to manufacture, traffic begins. As markets get wider and the merchant extends his activities, a larger circle of population is drawn together. When a ruler has intelligence enough to establish good systems of currency, transport and police, trade is encouraged, and that increases the unity of his dominions. Conversely, tariff-barriers, such as have recently been set up between the component parts of the late Austrian Empire, increase racial antagonism.

At present international trade, so far as tariff-barriers allow it to exist, is powerful in drawing the nations of Europe together. A large part of the commercial community depends for its prosperity upon foreign trade, and is therefore favourable to the preservation of peace in Europe. In 1914 this combining influence was overcome by the disruptive forces of militarism and race-hatred, and is still not yet fully restored. The friends of peace must wish earnestly to see trade throughout Europe in full activity once more. Such a powerful utilitarian influence will give support to the idealists who hope to see the civilized nations of the world working together in good-will.

Most of the work, which is done in connection with government and trade, is done obviously from non-moral motives; mainly from ambition and love of gain. Nevertheless, effective service in these fields has a moral value in so far as it establishes conditions which make a good moral life possible. There are many men who keep this fact in view when they surrender themselves to the preoccupations of worldly business; and this gives some moral dignity to lives which otherwise would be painfully prosaic and hard.

Religion also is a combining agency, in so far as it leads to the establishment of religious institutions or churches. The influence of churches, viewed merely as institutions, can be distinguished from that of the doctrines which they inculcate. The need of an inclusive religious system or church was felt acutely in the ancient world. The Greek polytheism, which makes so various and picturesque a show, was really a national calamity, because it aggravated the native separatism of the Greek race. The Romans in the pagan period did what they could towards establishing a world-church: the best of them adopted Stoicism; while for the benefit of the common people they promoted emperor-worship. What religion can do to unify people is shown strikingly by the career of Mahomet, who by imposing a uniform religious system upon the discordant Arab tribes, converted them into a powerful nation.

The fact that a religion is inclusive and recognizes no barriers of race, or caste, or social status is almost as important as the character of its doctrine. The civilization of the world has gained enormously by the inclusiveness of Christianity, which regards all human souls as having the same intrinsic value. Much of this good quality was lost at the Reformation. Against the obvious moral gain which we owe to the Reformation must be set the drawback that the Christian Church then split up into a multiplicity of hostile sects. The fissiparous tendency has been manifested especially in England; where in spite of much official repression many small sects have been formed, which have regarded all other religious bodies with suspicion or contempt, even though they might not differ seriously in doctrine. Persons interested in religious progress have marvelled at the sect-forming tendency and deplored it. Its deepest cause seems to me to be the old tribal spirit which impels men everywhere to form cliques and exclusive bodies, if they have any excuse for doing so. Religious separatism is plainly declining in our country; and in any case it does no serious harm, because there are so many other influences making for union. But we can see the malignity of its influence in Ireland, a country where tribalism is still very strong and where men seem to be greatly tempted by nature to hate each other.

Law can exercise a great combining influence in a country where there exists a uniform legal system administered impartially by judges without respect to race or social status. In constructing their law and judicial system the Romans made their greatest contribution to civilization. Quarrels are always arising in every society from various accidents and failings of human nature; and if not settled, they become aggravated into feuds and vendettas. When a man who is aggrieved finds that justice is denied to him, he becomes embittered against the social and political system under which he lives, and resolves to redress his wrongs with his own hand. And this is fatal to political unity and social good-will. It was justice in the main which held the Roman Empire together; as it was want of justice

which made the Athenian Empire so ready to
fall to pieces.

§ 2. Now let us consider institutions which
are directly moral. First take custom. It is so
unorganized that one is stretching language,
perhaps, in calling it an institution as a whole;
but many separate customs are definite enough
to deserve the name. In part custom is non-
moral, consisting of ways of behaviour which
have no more moral significance than the habits
of other gregarious creatures, such as dogs and
bees. But part of it is moral, because it shows
disinterested appreciation of man.

Those who have studied savages carefully are
always impressed by the moral element in
primitive society. The customs of savages are
full of respect and reverence for such things as
fall within their ken—the tribe, family relationships, justice as between tribesmen, gods and
ancestors. The range of valuation is enlarged
as men progress generally in culture.

In advanced societies custom is relatively less

important than among savages; because so much of our life is now fully organized and guided by reflection. We see its influence most clearly perhaps among boys, who are in so many respects at the barbarian level. A convenient case for study is that of custom at some English public school, Rugby for example, as it is depicted in *Tom Brown's Schooldays*. Many of the Rugby customs were evidently non-moral— mere local peculiarities of dress and manner, or dictated by utility. Sometimes they were anti-moral, as when Tom was 'roasted' by some elder boys at the dormitory fire; but in great part they were moral. The moral quality of the school-life at Rugby is in fact the chief cause of the popularity of Judge Hughes' book. The importance of school customs for moral education is shown by the anxiety of judicious head-masters to establish good customs and discourage bad ones. Boys are great sticklers for custom, or 'tradition' as it is generally called; and they can be influenced for good by means of it. By tradition qualities of public spirit, leadership and sportsmanlike fairness can be inculcated, and many others beside.

Those who can sympathize with boys find it easy to understand savages. Some savage customs are horrible or disgusting, cannibalism for example; but many of them express moral convictions. The very elaborate marriage regulations of the Australian blacks are intended to prevent incest. And even a non-moral custom— some peculiarity of dress or house-building— may be kept up by simple people, not from mere mental inertia, but from a feeling of respect for the good men of the past who followed that style.

The improvement of custom in a society is very like that of law, which will be mentioned presently, and consists in extending good treatment to classes and persons who previously received scant consideration. These are mostly persons who are more or less defenceless, especially strangers, women and children. Each of these classes has good qualities in actuality or potentiality, but not in actuality the qualities of the able-bodied tribesman. In the simplest societies it is the tribesmen who are supreme in matters of custom; because hunting and war, the tribesman's occupations, are those of supreme importance. And so the customs of the simplest societies are unfavourable to those who can neither hunt nor fight. Schools can be utilized once more to illustrate the improvement of custom. In English schools of 80 years ago—the Tom Brown period—new boys were liable to much ill-treatment, merely because they were new-comers; whereas at the present day in one school of my acquaintance a custom has been established by which new boys are exempt for their first term from all molestation, until they 'feel their feet' in their new surroundings. Similarly there has been a great improvement in the treatment of the younger boys by the elder. Junior boys are no longer liable to be 'roasted' at Rugby.

Speaking in philosophical terms one may say that the improvement of custom consists in a wider and deeper valuation of human qualities. In a clannish society the fact that a person is not of the clan is enough to set people against him; in a rude society the fact that he is wanting in physical force is enough to make people overlook any gifts or potentialities which he may possess. The removal of these faults is hardly possible without changes in the community's general way of life. Strangers will always be disliked so long as men live in little independent tribes. Weaklings will always be despised in a society where there is no culture, and where hunting and fighting are all-important. When states are formed and wealth accumulated, men come to value other gifts and graces and appreciate those who manifest them.

Law is an institution which is full of morality; it is a great mistake to regard the laws of one's country as a load of restrictions upon freedom. In the future the volume of law will be much greater than now, because the state will be more complex, and will be more carefully organized for happiness and virtue. But the ordinary man will feel no addition to his burden; on the contrary, he will recognize that owing to the laws he has more opportunities of personal expansion. Now, laws give expression to the growing moral convictions of the community, establishing institutions by which good purposes may be carried into effect, and providing only as an unpleasant necessity for the punishment of transgressors. In this spirit do the majority of our citizens regard the laws; and that is why the British are the most law-abiding of peoples. Generally the enactment of a law suffices to effect its main purpose. If Parliament passes an act forbidding secret commissions or establishing a weekly half-holiday for shop-assistants, this is regarded throughout the country as an authoritative moral pronouncement which every decent citizen is bound to respect.

The development of any great system of law, such as the Roman or English, is deeply interesting to the moralist. In Rome we see how the labours of a succession of jurists, at first native and later cosmopolitan, enlarged the narrow old jural ideas of Rome till they became adequate to defining the civil relationships of civilized citizens without reference to race or creed. The growth of English law is going on before our eyes. The principles which we have inherited from the remote past are being developed by the decisions of the Courts; and, when new principles are needed, Acts of Parliament establish them.

A good example of the way in which the growth of English law shows moral progress is to be found in the changes which have taken place in the legal status of women. The principles of our common law in this respect are a compromise between the customs of Teutonic barbarians, who thought little of women, and the tenets of Christianity, which has always defended the weaker members of the community. In course of time Englishmen have come to see that the common law does not give women as much as they deserve; and a series of enactments, of which the Sex Disqualification Act is the last, have given expression to convictions which are primarily of a moral order. We should mistake the nature of these convictions, if we regarded them as expressions of commiseration; they are rather expressions of appreciation—appreciation of the very valuable qualities which women possess, not merely for domestic life, but also for the management of the commonwealth.

Education is well recognized, in this country at least, as being no less important for morals than for intellectual training. This is plain enough, if only we give an adequately full meaning to the term 'morality.' In its current use morality has too much the sense of restriction; it ought primarily to mean appreciation. The business of the educator is to help the pupil to understand and love the world. Reviewing the history of education, we can see in what respects it has been wanting at different times and how reformers have improved it. The Roman education was narrow according to our ideas; it consisted predominantly of rhetoric (in preparation for a forensic career) with some study of Latin and Greek literature. It strikes us as being alienated from the simpler aspects of human nature, and as disregarding many of the things which bring joy and sorrow to ordinary men. Medieval education was narrower still. It was so much bound up with the interests, prejudices and special ideas of the clerical class; a class, which because of its exclusion from family life, was deprived of the most amiable and humanizing interests which men enjoy. The Renascence was a rediscovery of man; it was an emancipation and a revelation of the value of neglected things. It brought into a liberal education subjects which ought never to be excluded from it—passion, romance and the spirit of bold adventure in things sacred and profane.

Within the last two generations there has been yet another movement of expansion. The study of classics had hardened and narrowed and grown inhuman. Scholars pored upon the old literature with an interest limited mainly to its verbal form; they did not reconstruct the ancient life by imagination, or bring the ancient literature into relation with the problems of modern society; they treated natural science with contempt, and neglected the literature of modern Europe. But recently many new subjects of study have been introduced which have not withdrawn energy from the old subjects, but have caused men to study them with wider understanding. The scholar, and the educator who diffuses the scholar's ideas, look out upon the world with a much wider range of sympathy. The intellectual gain is manifest; but we must recognize also that there is no less a gain in morality.

Religion is, of course, a great moral institution. It exercises a moralizing influence by means of rules and precepts which have become invested with religious sanctity; the Decalogue, for example. But still more powerful, perhaps, in relation to conduct are the conceptions of the divine character which are current among those who believe in the religion. The deities of low-grade savages are not so much gods as petty devils, inspiring continual fear and needing continually petty propitiations; like the fairies which darken the lives of the peasantry in the wilder parts of Ireland. Even the Olympian gods were full of faults, as Plato complains in the *Republic*; scarce a form of transgression but could be palliated by some example from those unedifying ancient legends. As men improve, they think as Plato thought about old gods. A god represents the ideal of the generation which formed the conception of him. And ideals go out of date; nay, they even become abhorrent to a later generation. We see this very plainly in Greek literature. In several plays of Euripides the gods are represented in the most odious light; in the *Ion*, *Hercules Furens* and *Hippolytus*, for example, Apollo, Here and Aphrodite are no better than malignant demons. Euripides was stronger in criticism than in construction so far as regards religion, and he does not make much contribution towards a better theology. But we find high conceptions of the gods in Sophocles and Plato. I do not wish to enter here into a full explanation of the moral superiority of Christianity to paganism; but two points may be noticed. In Christian teaching there is much more recognition of the humbler and gentler virtues: originally the religion was emphatically a poor man's religion; and it is also very favourable to women, especially in its Catholic form. The divine beings, to whom the attention of Christian worshippers is mainly directed, are Christ and, in Catholicism, the Blessed Virgin; it is hardly necessary to say that they embody many valuable elements which are not to be found in pagan deities. And thus they have enlarged the range of moral appreciation throughout the world.

§ 3. The government of an advanced country ought in all its departments, national and local, to manifest a very wide appreciation of human nature. It is a mistake to think that the work of a government should be limited to governing; it has moral duties also, which become more important the further the community progresses in civilization.

A civilized state cannot be governed satisfactorily unless the governing class has wide appreciations. Among uncultured men the appreciations of the governing class are necessarily narrow; in a hunting society the best hunters will take the lead in everything, in a warlike society the best warriors. In our own wealth-seeking society leadership tends to fall into the hands of wealthy men.

Governments composed exclusively of wealthy men, as most oligarchies are, always show narrow-mindedness. At the best they value only some special elements of character, those which conduce to wealth-getting; at the worst they can hardly be said to value character at all, but are merely sottish and grasping. A truly democratic government should be differently inspired; we may expect to see it organize the commonwealth in a spirit of catholic human valuation. Above all it will lay stress upon the ordinary virtues of ordinary citizens.

In conformity with this spirit in the governing class, there will be in a good political community many institutions which aim specifically at promoting the welfare of the majority of the citizens; while all the institutions of the community will be arranged with some reference to the welfare of the majority. We in England are still far from possessing all the institutions which are used; but we have many more than in the days of oligarchic domination. Eighteenth-century England was very poor in institutions; our rulers certainly performed more or less efficiently the elementary functions of government, but paid little heed to the moral welfare of the population. Such institutions as existed were not of good quality; they were not contrived so as to produce good results, having regard to the needs and the psychological character of mankind. For example, in education very little was done by the government, and such public or semi-public institutions as existed were full of stupidities and corruptions. We have now many more educational institutions and of a better quality; but we may expect to see great advances in the future when our commonwealth has been fully democratized.

We may take educational institutions as an example to illustrate the moral spirit by which governments and political institutions should be animated. A truly democratic educational policy is one which assumes that every class of citizens is well worth educating. A truly democratic state will set up such educational institutions as the welfare of the people may seem to need, or will encourage and regulate such institutions as may already exist. It will recommend courses of study which will help men to a wide appreciation of human things; it will make arrangements for inculcating virtue, not so much by preaching as by practice and example; above all it will take care that the ordinary virtues are strongly insisted upon, because the more brilliant qualities are better able to look after themselves.

When such a policy is pursued in all the branches of action which a government undertakes, it greatly improves the morality of the citizens. The chief influence will be exercised merely by the spectacle of good principles embodied in clearly apprehensible form. This is so with every institution. For example, the moral effect of a school upon its pupils is not mainly due to the inculcation of moral precepts; most English educators are inclined to shrink from direct inculcation. It is due to the mere fact that the pupils live as members of an institution which is manifestly constructed and worked upon a good plan. Through the influence of a sort of suggestion they adopt similar principles for the guidance of their own lives; and they are able to devote themselves wholeheartedly to the service of the institution.

§ 4. The spirit of human valuation which animates the institutions of a good common life—customs, laws, religion and government—should find expression in literature and art. The moral importance of literature and art is not adequately recognized in our country. I know that in the main these things exist in order to cheer and amuse us. But they have also a great moral function, inasmuch as it is the business of artists and literary men to put the moral aspirations of the age into forms which will make their way easily into men's hearts. And the commonwealth by means of institutions should accord recognition to the function.

At present our country is poor in literary and artistic institutions of any kind; as for institutions of this character supported by public authority, we can hardly say that they exist. I wish to argue that such institutions should be established. Surely every civilized country should have a Ministry of Fine Arts which should take within its scope the moral improvement of literary and artistic production. I will try to indicate some of the ways in which a wholesome influence might be exercised upon literature by public agency. What is said about literature will apply, with necessary changes, to the arts in general.

In the world of literature there is no lack of evils which need powerful agencies to correct them. Writers are influenced adversely by the same sort of causes as ordinary men: they are discouraged by neglect and penury, and are demoralized by excessive or capricious rewards; they succumb to the ordinary temptations of commercial life. Commercialism is the worst influence upon literature just now. Literary men suffer greatly from the fact that, in respect of money, they stand upon the same footing as the ordinary adventurer. When a man has written a book, he does not know what he is going to receive; it may be much or it may be nothing. Sometimes an inferior book is extravagantly rewarded, sometimes a good book gets no reward. In order to secure a living wage a writer must scheme and measure his wits against those of tradesmen; sometimes he resorts to acts of advertisement and public posing; if successful, he is tempted into vicious habits of over-production.

For the encouragement of good literature it is not necessary that there should be great pecuniary rewards. In ancient Athens the material remuneration of literary men was inadequate, perhaps altogether wanting; but the general tone of society was elevated, there was much good taste which was expressed through authoritative channels, and there was plenty of honour for excellent work. This explains why a single Greek city could produce that wonderful abundance of tragic and comic dramas, a few specimens of which have come down to us. The conditions of dramatic production were dignified and pure. The plays were produced at national festivals associated with patriotism and religion; there was no pushing and bargaining with managers; the atmosphere of the theatre was not, as it is in France at least to-day, polluted with mercenary vice; the merit of the pieces was judged by the best judges that could be found. Unsubstantial as the rewards of the Athenian theatre may seem to us, they were enough to stimulate play-wrights to the highest productivity.

The theatre has always been a powerful agent for inculcating moral ideas; in spite of many various maladjustments due to neglect and stupidity, it accomplishes some good in modern England. But we do not trouble to use even those means of elevating the stage which are current in other nations. Every considerable German town has a municipal theatre, which prides itself upon maintaining a high artistic level. We care for none of these things; we are the Gallios of the arts.

The theatre is the case where institutions are needed most to raise the moral tone of literature; but the governments of the future, if they have morality at heart, will give their care to every sort of literature and every sort of productive art by which moral ideas can be set before the world. There should be suitable means of producing works to the public, and of encouraging the authors of good work with rewards and honours which will not corrupt them.

These things and many more will be attempted, let us hope, in the future; I quite admit that it would be premature to attempt them all now. Literature must always conform to the taste of the leading class. Now the leading class in European society is to a large extent parasitic; so many of its members are idle and useless, and therefore full of the silly fancies which beset idle, useless minds. The class is wealth-demoralized, and so its literature is wealth-demoralized also. As society, growing more earnest and practical, clears itself from its present taint, public agency may intervene gradually to raise the tone of literature.

CHAPTER III

THE PRINCIPLE IN THE VIRTUES

§ 1. The theory of my essay can be supported, I think, by reviewing the virtues. It seems to me that, psychologically, the basis of any particular virtue is appreciation of a certain class of objects, which are human beings or human qualities. When men learn to value the objects, they acquire the virtue. The process of acquiring the ordinary range of virtues I call moralization.

Moralization can be studied from the individual standpoint, or from the racial. Individual moralization is nearest to us; it can be observed indeed wherever there are children. Children begin as non-moral creatures, and are moralized by education. The moralization of the race is more remote: to study it we need the light of history; indeed, much of it is prehistoric and can be conjectured only with the help of observations upon existing savages. And yet racial moralization is easier to understand: it follows a general plan, the outlines of which are clear enough; whereas individual moralization is influenced so much by varying circumstances. In the main I will speak of the virtues as they appear at the successive stages of race-development.

Looking at moralization in this way we can see its gradations. Man begins with a narrow range of appreciation, corresponding to his limited social outlook and his limited powers of mind; as his opportunities broaden and his powers increase, he values new things, without ceasing to care for the old. It is possible to say what are the more elementary and what are the more advanced virtues, because we can say what objects come naturally within the range of simple men, and to what objects they naturally advance. And, before our remote anthropoid ancestors acquired morality at all, there must have been a pre-moral stage.

Before trying to distinguish the stages of

moralization, let us consider for a moment the pre-conditions of morality. There can be no approach to morality without a gregarious way of life. Solitary creatures are merely selfish, and take no notice of each other except as enemies. But gregarious creatures by living and acting together come to like each other's society, and acquire a sympathetic power which makes them understand each other. Friendliness and sympathy are greatly increased when animals co-operate or help each other in getting food and other tasks. There must have been a time when our simian ancestors had no more morality than monkeys have to-day. But monkey-like creatures which are gregarious, and which co-operate rather more than existing monkeys, seem to be in a position in which morality might be expected to arise.

Anthropology puts forward some probable conjectures as to how our simian ancestors developed into men; they were, it seems, apelike creatures who took to hunting. They lived in small groups or packs, inhabiting caves and feeding upon game. The ancient cave-men of Europe have left many silent records behind them, and we get light also from the analogy of low-grade savages still existing. Now there are two kinds of moral feeling which would be very useful to such creatures, devotion to leaders and devotion to the interests of the pack. I put forward the conjecture that morality first came into being when the subordinate hunter obeyed his leader, not merely with a doglike submission, but with some feeling of admiration for the leader's excellence—his strength, courage, sagacity and general serviceableness; and also when the members of the pack, both leaders and led, felt a sentiment directed towards the pack—some sort of admiration for it, not mere doglike gregariousness.

Virtues make their appearance in a society as they are needed for the welfare of the society. The earliest of the virtues I take to be tribal loyalty, which has both a personal and a communal form. Perhaps the personal form is earlier; it needs less understanding to be loyal to a person than to a community. But even among the lower savages we find some communal loyalty; and among the higher savages it is more impressive than the personal kind. Consider the loyalty to his tribe of the Red Indian under torture when captured by his enemies. The two kinds of loyalty usually reinforce each other: the leader is honoured, not only for what he is in himself, but also for his tribal position; while the tribal ordinances are revered because they embody the wisdom of ancient leaders.

Among children of civilized peoples there is much barbarism, because they 'throw back' to an earlier stage of culture. Together with some of the faults of barbarians they have many of their good qualities. Now, loyalty is one of the most conspicuous of boyish virtues.

All this enables us to say what are the elementary virtues; they are loyalty and the qualities which are necessary to make loyal feeling effective. They are the virtues of good tribesmen; the qualities which enable men to excel in leadership, in devotion to leaders, and in hearty co-operation with comrades.

Distinguished among the elementary virtues is pride. There are various sorts of pride, and some of them border upon vice; so pride has got a bad name, but upon the whole it is a virtue. Its basis is the desire to be well thought of by one's neighbours. A loyal tribesman naturally wins the approval of his tribe; and when he knows this and resolves to maintain the standard of conduct which has earned approval, he is proud. Pride is a great virtue of warriors; they are ashamed of showing cowardice, and fiercely resent imputations on their courage. In some respects pride may seem to be opposed to another military virtue, that of obedience. But that is not so among civilized fighting men, where the limits of authority are well defined. There is such a thing as proud obedience;

recruits of the British Army are expected to acquire soldierly pride as well as habits of discipline.

Another famous elementary virtue is courage. It belongs especially to leaders who have to set a good example in hunting dangerous game and in war. Hence it is glorified above all other virtues in ancient song and story.

Veracity is closely akin to courage and pride. Men lie, mostly, because they are afraid; certainly, the unwarlike races of the world are inferior to the fighting races in the telling of truth. The other motive to lying is desire of gain. A proud man will resist both these temptations; he just states the facts, and lets the other party think what he will. Veracity is necessary for tribal confidence. A good leader does not deceive, nor does a good subordinate.

Fidelity is the characteristic virtue of subordinates and comrades. It is greatly esteemed in simple, warlike societies, such as medieval England, where the name of 'traitor' was the deepest of insults. And the faithful must be staunch—'good at need,' not shaken by danger, and not growing tired with lapse of time.

For these primitive virtues men need an endowment of instinct, especially for loyalty and courage. A man is incapable of loyalty who is anti-gregarious; who congenitally dislikes society and prefers to live apart, like a 'lone' wolf or a 'rogue' elephant. Nor can a man be courageous if fear has naturally a paralyzing or very painful effect upon him. But instinctive qualities do not become virtues till they are subordinated to and transformed by a rational human principle. Ability to fight, to lead and to follow cannot deserve moral approbation, unless a man has an unselfish admiration for the social system to which he belongs and for the persons who take a leading position in it.

In savage societies, where the men live so much in public, the tribal virtues are inculcated without reflection from early boyhood. In our own society everybody lives much more at home; and the child comes first into contact with the domestic virtues. The inculcation of the tribal virtues has to be delayed till the child is brought into a wider circle. Schools are the chief places where manliness is taught, and this is one of the reasons why schools are so necessary, and why a home education is no proper education at all. The tribal virtues are those which boys appreciate most. Education has made great progress in England during the last fifty years, and part of our gain consists in recognizing the moral needs of boys. Boys need institutions, chiefly of an athletic character, towards which they can feel devotion, and which they can serve in strenuous and self-sacrificing ways; and they need bold leaders whom they can admire. There are not sufficient opportunities for practising the harder virtues in the sheltered home-life of English upper-class families.

§ 2. Domestic virtues are not possible till men have made some progress towards civilization.

We do not find them among wandering hunters of small game; but they begin to appear whenever agriculture or other means of obtaining wealth enables men to take up a settled way of life and to live in houses. They depend upon appreciation of home, and of the personal qualities which make a satisfactory home-life possible.

The domestic virtues are primarily qualities of woman. The domestic woman is one who values home: she likes a fixed habitation in which a clean and orderly life can be lived, and which can be beautified; and she is fond of children, not merely with the attachment of the animal-mother, but as persons to be trained in virtue, and to be 'kept nice' and adorned so that they can be objects of legitimate pride.

In man the domestic virtues are secondary, because they depend mainly on valuing the domestic qualities in woman and in appreciating the kind of home and family life which only a woman can make possible for him. In countries where wealth is both abundant and well diffused, women have good opportunities of developing their characteristic gifts and graces. They are then much esteemed and their opinions respected, so that a high level of domestic virtue prevails throughout the society.

Those who have studied the theory of morals are not likely to make the obvious mistake of over-emphasizing the negative or prohibitional side of domestic virtue. Prohibitions are easy to formulate, and they naturally appear first when moral precepts are put into definite form. It requires less intelligence to say "Thou shalt not steal" than to explain the moral value of using property wisely. So with domestic virtue. Conjugal infidelity is a vice, because it breaks up a home; it outrages the primitive feeling of sexual jealousy, and makes a harmonious married life impossible, or at least very difficult. But for people who have no home and no appreciation of home-life the Seventh Commandment loses much of its meaning.

§ 3. The civic or political virtues are more

than the tribal, because the state is much more than the tribe. Tribal feeling is an excellent thing for primitive men, and it is necessary to lead on to later virtues; but it makes neighbouring clans hate each other, whereas the state brings them together. And a state, so far as it is good, not only gives men opportunities for cultivating the wider and finer virtues, but itself exemplifies them. The state therefore can be regarded with an appreciation much higher than that which can be directed towards the tribe, and this appreciation is the basis of political virtue.

The state is, of course, by far the most important of political or civic organizations; it is supremely important for defence and it also should do more than any other institution to help the citizens to lead a good and dignified life. But minor civic associations within the state can conduce to the same purposes, and should be objects of corresponding valuations. Cities should be organized in such a way as to promote the moral welfare of the citizens, who on their side should respond with feelings of municipal patriotism.

The opportunities of men for developing political virtue must increase as institutions improve. A state which is full of evil influences, like France under the old regime, can evoke nothing more than an inferior kind of patriotism; nor can there be any proper civic feeling in cities such as English cities were before the reform of our municipal system. Everyone admits that English political and civic institutions are still very imperfect; when they are better, we shall have a higher level of political virtue in our citizens.

Patriotism has fallen into some disrepute, because it can be so easily counterfeited and exploited for bad ends. In Europe the kings of old time, when they quarrelled with neighbouring kings for dynastic or even merely personal reasons, used to embroil their subjects in war and stir up racial hatred, and then appeal for help in men and money on grounds of patriotism. To us now this seems detestable trickery. Patriotism has been discredited too by being associated with vulgar boasting. It is unpleasing to hear men claiming admiration for their country on the ground that it is very big— the sun never sets on it; or is mistress of the seas; or, worst of all, that it is very rich. Legitimate matters of pride are quite different; that the state embodies principles of good morality, that the citizens have a high standard of private virtue, and that an excellent culture is diffused through every class. These are things for which nations are justly admired; though, from the nature of the case, it is impossible to boast about them. Men of the highest character will gladly serve such a state, content with moderate rewards, and getting their main satisfaction from the pride of co-operating in so admirable an institution.

§ 4. With the modern development of international co-operation and intercourse there has come into being a new kind of international virtue which was unknown to our forefathers. It consists partly in appreciation of the qualities of man as man; but mainly in appreciation of the special features of national character and gifts which have been developed in various lands. Some minds take an interest in human varieties, just as others are attracted by birds or flowers. In the literature, life and manners of such a country as France there is plenty to engage the admiration of an intelligent Englishman, who has emancipated himself from the primitive tribal prejudice which makes him dislike all foreigners impartially. It is because of these new sentiments of international good-will that men to-day are ready to enter into schemes which aim at the general welfare of mankind irrespective of race.

There have not been many great internationalists in the past; perhaps this kind of virtue does not lead often to individual distinction. I do not mention the missionaries of Christianity and other world-religions, because their inter-

nationalism was of a special kind. Among modern
secular friends of man Nobel and Carnegie
deserve mention. At present the great practical
outcome of this spirit is to be seen in the League
of Nations. The Covenant of the League and
Part XIII of the Treaty of Versailles, which
establishes an International Labour Organization purposing to raise the conditions of the
working-classes throughout the world, are most
impressive manifestations of the international
spirit, and will be regarded in the future as
marking an epoch in the moral progress of
mankind.

Schemes of international welfare, such as those
associated with the League, are usually recom-
mended to us on the ground of their utility.
It is pointed out, very justly, that civilized
nations are now so interdependent that one
nation cannot suffer without bringing suffering
upon the rest; and that one cannot rise much in
the scale of culture unless the others also are
raised. This, of course, is a sensible and effective

way of recommending international schemes. But would such utilitarian arguments have much effect without the appeal of sentimental interests, which we feel deeply but do not desire to talk about? For example, do Englishmen who know nothing of the French language and literature really feel much interest in the welfare of France? I doubt it. Such a moral advance seems hardly possible without a correspondent broadening of intellectual appreciation.

§ 5. The foregoing are worldly virtues, the common factor in which is human valuation. I wish now to speak of religious virtue, and to inquire if the same principle can be discerned there also. The inquiry must be undertaken, because so many teachers have said that religion directs our thoughts towards a totally different sphere, and should make us insensible to mundane affairs. According to my theory a man is the more virtuous, the deeper his interest is in the world, and the more strongly he appreciates the admirable elements in it. But, if religion makes a man turn away from the world, there must be a formidable antithesis between worldly and other-worldly virtue. Does such an antithesis really exist? My argument will be that it is quite imaginary. Religion, so far as it can be called virtuous, is inspired by the same principle as worldly virtue; progress in worldly virtue leads on naturally to religious virtue.

Originally, there seems to have been very little moral quality in religion. There is nothing morally laudable in the magical practices of savages, by which they seek to ensure their food-supply or to injure their enemies; nor can we sympathize much with the worship which is paid to a god who is honoured by his worshippers merely as a sender of rain or as an ally against hostile tribes. The lower we descend in exploring the levels of culture, the less we admire the gods. At the lowest level they are nothing better than petty malignant spirits, which have to be placated but are not loved.

The status of the gods is raised concurrently

with advance in political organization. Unregimented savages have gods which are very local and very circumscribed in their activity. The gods gain a wider range as government advances. When city-states and nation-states come into existence, we find men worshipping 'high' gods, who occupy in the spiritual sphere a position analogous to that of the king. When a high god is thoroughly established in a state, the smaller tribal or local gods are either violently suppressed, as happened in Arabia; or they are worshipped as subordinate deities, as happened in Greece and Rome.

The political causes which lead to the establishment of high gods are hardly of a moral character; but high gods can easily be moralized. Citizens who are disposed in favour of virtue find help in regarding the gods as supporters of moral rules. A morally good god is also an object which can be revered; men need such objects the more, the further they advance in culture. The first objects of human reverence

are the community and its leaders. In some parts
of eastern Europe this state of feeling still sur-
vives, unless the Russian Revolution has de-
stroyed it. The Russian peasant was wont to
say: "The voice of the *mir* (village community)
is the voice of God"; and he reverenced the
Tsar as semi-divine. But, at a further stage of
progress, mundane objects become inadequate
for the better sort of men; even village communities are seen to be imperfect, and kings
still more so. Earnest souls, therefore, take up
the super-mundane objects which religion sup-
plies to them and invest them with moral
attributes, which grow higher as the moral
consciousness of the society advances. The conceptions of deity thus formed are fixed and
perpetuated by tradition, scripture and ritual.
Certain figures of religion, the Buddha for
example, attract the reverence of devout men
throughout long ages. And so they come to
have a powerful reactive influence upon moral
principles and practice.

The importance of good conceptions of deity for spiritual welfare justifies the great efforts which have been made to secure religious reform. Churches are intensely conservative and cling to sacred books and traditions long after they have ceased to be in harmony with the needs of the age, and even after they have become an offence to enlightened minds. The process of 'eliminating and decrassifying' ancient faiths is always going on, but it is very slow and imperfect. Great religious changes can hardly be effected suddenly without a violent social convulsion, accompanied with much bloodshed and suffering.

We may say in general terms, then, that the kind of religion which is morally valuable has grown out of superstition, which is morally neutral. In some minds, which are religious in the best sense, elements of superstition still survive. Many a good man thinks it prudent, when salt is spilt, to throw a pinch over his left shoulder; or he shudders when he sees two knives crossed upon the table-cloth. Such relics of primitive belief do not affect our moral estimate of him, though they may make us think less of his understanding.

There is yet another element in religion which is not definitely moral, though it stands much higher than superstition; I mean the element of mysticism. This consists in a feeling of union or communion with a world-spirit, which the mystic believes to be behind the appearances of the world of phenomena. The sense of cosmic union is manifestly the chief thing in typical mystics like Spinoza and Amiel. It is not the same as the moral kind of religion, because many virtuously religious people are not at all mystical; while some mystics, such as the Anabaptists, are well known to have been deficient in morality. Spinoza also is very emphatic about the moral indifference of 'Nature or God.' The mystic, in fact, does not want to be united with God because God is moral, but because he is cosmic.

We may conclude then that there is no element in religion which is in opposition to the principle of human value. Superstition, on the whole, seems to be rather injurious to morals; but this is because it belongs altogether to a low plane of culture. Mysticism, on the other hand, seems favourable to morality; not because it affirms the moral principle, but because it is connected with a very wide outlook upon the world. It may drain away a man's energies from morality, but seems more likely to enhance them. The moral element in religion consists in appreciation of a morally good God, whose goodness is not alien to that which we find among men. The religious man cannot be termed virtuous unless he feels this appreciation.

The difference which distinguishes the moral element in religion from ordinary worldly morality lies in a difference in the objects which are valued respectively. In the feelings of devotion which men entertain towards the tribe, the family and the state, the objects are real, or at least partially real. In patriotism the object which is valued—England or France—has a reality which is guaranteed by perception; though, certainly, for the English patriot England must be symbolized somehow and idealized, and cannot be England just as it is with all its dirt and poverty. But in the devotion of religion the objects are mainly ideal. I do not mean of course that God has no existence; or that important religious personages, such as Gotama, were not historical. I only mean that as objects of moral admiration they are ideal beings or mainly ideal. No one has learnt by perceptual observation the moral qualities of deity; nor are the excellences which are attributed by Buddhists to Gotama recorded in authentic histories. But this ideality does not impair the reality of religious sentiments or weaken their influence upon conduct.

§ 6. So far I have said nothing about the critical side of virtue; and yet in morality, as in every other pursuit, an agent is incomplete unless he can criticize. For the work of everyday conduct it is necessary that a man should judge the people around him, and himself also in relation to his moral performance. But I am thinking rather of men who are capable of general criticism; who can understand the principles which are implicit in the chief institutions of their society and can think of improvements. Such a capacity belongs only to those who are well-instructed and mature; we do not look for it in the very young whose business is with assimilating principles rather than with criticism, or in people of simple societies who are not trained in reflection.

In what consists the virtuousness of criticism? It is a fine experience, certainly, and gives much satisfaction to the agent. But is there any duty in it? I think there is; because it implies devotion to an ideal. The true critic imagines a better condition of human nature than what he finds existing; and this is his inspiration and criterion. This is what distinguishes the critic from the mere grumbler. The grumbler has a grievance, or fancies that he has one; the shoe pinches him and he breaks out into protest. Usually he has no remedy at all to suggest. But the critic always has a better state of things before his mental view.

In the past some of the most famous idealists and critics have devoted themselves to the reform of religion. The successful ones founded new institutions; and we can understand most easily what was in their minds by comparing the new institutions with those which they superseded. The early Christians who revolted against the harshness and impurity of pagan society put the best of their souls into their church; and so did the Protestants who revolted against Catholicism in the sixteenth century. I see no essential difference between these reformers and those who are merely secular and wish to change the mundane features of society without touching religion. They seem both to be kinds of idealists who desire the improvement of man.

If this is so, criticism is for the best and ablest characters not only a duty but a right, and is necessary for the full development of moral experience. A man who has critical faculty craves opportunity for its exercise; he wishes to practise it, like any other virtue. If opportunities of criticism are denied him, if he is persecuted or terrorized into silence, he has a painful sense of repression and loss.

Under favourable conditions the reformer may manifest great spiritual energy, and become a shining example to the world. When an able man has formed in his mind a scheme of things which is better than what he sees existing and sets to work to get it realized, possibly against dangerous and unscrupulous opponents, very powerful psychological motives come into play, which greatly develop his character and lift him far above the ordinary plane of life. In some conspicuous cases, Martin Luther for example, the reformer astonishes the world by his devotion to an ideal; and, presenting great moral thoughts in a shape which attracts the devotion of ordinary men, raises the whole tone of his age.

A social critic may be enthusiastic and yet not altogether in the right. He will avoid mistakes only so far as his ideal is inspired by a right moral principle. If he adopts as his chief principle something which is mistaken, his ideal will be faulty; he will judge wrongly, condemning where he ought to praise or tolerate, and praising where he ought to condemn. Usually these wrong ideals concur with some natural defect of character in the agent. For example, there are men who are too authoritative and rigid, and these are naturally inclined to an ethical system which makes the most of law and regards obedience to it as the main element of virtue. Laws are of necessity rigorous: they must be formulated in precise language with a minimum of exceptions and reservations; they cannot recognize fine shades of purpose and complex circumstances. Kant is an extreme example of an authoritative moralist. His system is so severe that he thought himself justified in saying that in all probability no human being had ever performed a truly moral action. On the other hand there are natures which are too soft and yielding, and cannot show sternness when sternness is really needed. It is possible to give way too much to the pleasures of charity, and this fault is encouraged if we make benevolence our chief principle and criterion. The principle of Reason is too cold. Some highly intellectual people are deficient in the ordinary passions and affections of humanity. These are born Platonists; the highest thing in the world for them is a sort of mathematical enthusiasm, and they are quite out of touch with the motives which sway the lives of ordinary men. All these errors will be avoided, I think, by those who put the principle of human value into the foremost place.

The social critic needs some such criterion to enable him to judge the foundations of things. In ordinary, everyday moral judgments men use the standard of the society in which they live. This is common-sense. Common-sense people take things as they are, and judge men and actions as right or wrong according as they conduce to the prosperity of the society in the form in which it is established. Magistrates have this in their minds when they say in punishing offenders, "This conduct must be stopped in the public interest." They are taking for granted the principles which underlie the existing state of things. The philosopher must go deeper; his criticism may bring accepted principles into question. In the ancient world he was confronted with slavery and all the evils of a slave-society; in Victorian England there was the nineteenth-century commercialism which Carlyle and Ruskin attacked so fiercely. As a master-principle for his ideal he will be safe with the principle of human value. He will recognize the multitude of good human qualities, and the variety and flexibility of schemes of life; he will value individuals only in so far as they have something truly valuable in them; and he will see that high intelligence is only one of the many excellent qualities of man.

One who is resolved morally to do his best will not be satisfied with any ideal which recognizes no more than a part of human excellence. It is true that each of us has his limitations— limitations of intellect, of temperament and of opportunity; but we can do our best to transcend them. We can resolve not to shut our eyes to anything that is good; we cannot attain catholicity, but we can aspire to it. A critic of this kind will not fail in the critic's primary duty, that of pointing out defects in the existing system and suggesting something better in their place. Nor should he be wanting in good judgment, because his mind is not narrowed by prejudice or partiality.

CHAPTER IV

CULTURAL INTERESTS

§ 1. By 'cultural interests' I mean art, literature and science. They are not directly part of
morality; a man can live a morally good life
without proficiency in any of them. Nevertheless
they are closely related to morality. The re-
lationship consists in this, that the chief element
in them is an appreciation of human value closely
parallel to that which is displayed in morality.

First consider art, for the case is plainest there.
Plastic art had its origin in various motives
remote from morals; the most fundamental
perhaps was pride of workmanship. Man's
superiority over other creatures depends mainly
upon his possession of hands; and the 'handy'
man, the man who can do remarkable feats of
workmanship, has always been admired. Men
like to have before their eyes in hours of repose
representations of objects which belong to

pleasant interests of action; the mammoth-hunter prizes a drawing of the beast upon a piece of ivory, just as the sporting squire hangs pictures of fox-hunting in his dining-room. And so the skilful draughtsman has been honoured from the earliest times.

The growth of technical skill is encouraged by other motives. One belongs to magic and religion. Some of the earliest works of art, certainly the earliest paintings, have been found in dark caves very difficult of access, apparently untouched since they were put there by immemorial artists. As the purpose of these works could not have been public display, the presumption is that they were due to motives of magic or religion; perhaps to some idea of gaining power over the objects represented, or of placating gods. Later in history we know what a powerful stimulus to art was given by the Catholic Church, which utilized freely both the plastic and the musical arts to enhance the devotion of worshippers, and to magnify the glory of prelates. And we know what a blighting effect Mahommedanism has had upon the plastic arts in the East by borrowing the Second Commandment from Judaism.

Another powerful cause promoting the growth of art has been the desire of personal display. The most ancient motive impelling men and women to appear remarkable or beautiful is certainly sex. This is the origin of the bright colours and other adornments upon birds and animals; and this is the chief motive which makes men and women attentive to elegance of clothing. There is also much personal adornment for purposes of warlike show or political pomp. The elaborate workmanship of arms and accoutrements in Homer is due to this; and we can see the same thing in our own public ceremonies, such as a royal wedding or a state-opening of Parliament.

These are the chief of the early motives which make men produce works of plastic art, such as drawings, pictures and statuary. But as these arts grow to maturity, we find them pervaded more and more by a spirit of human valuation. Statuary is typical. Archaic statues are conventional or grotesque. Many of the Indian idols revolt us because they mishandle the human figure; their makers thought only of some idea or principle which seemed valuable to them, fertility for example symbolized by a female figure with many breasts. The early Greek sculptures are shapeless and unnatural; not so much because the carvers lacked skill, as because they were not interested in the human form for its own sake. Very different is the spirit of Greek statuary when the genius of the nation became mature. Motives of religion or display may have had their share in the work; but there can be no doubt that the purely human interest is supreme.

The plastic art of modern society is so various and subtle in its appeal that we may not realize how universally it is pervaded with humanity. Where, it may be asked, is the human element in pictures of mountain and sea? The answer is that we are interested in these things because they are connected with the life of man, or because they exhibit a life which we fancy to be of kindred quality to our own.

The argument about literature is very similar. Magic and religion had much to do with the origin of it; there were invocations and hymns to the gods, and sacred books containing tenets of religion with tales and histories illustrating them. Kingship also made its contribution; glory-loving rulers had records made of their achievements, and they paid minstrels to sing their praises. But, as soon as literature really 'gets going,' its chief motive is admiration of human excellence generally. The most primitive sort of literary works are folk-legends, such as the Kalevala, dealing with the exploits of a national hero. Wainamoinen in the Finnish epic represents the type which the people thought admirable in itself; he is celebrated without thought of religious doctrine or political advancement.

When literature is well-established, any one can see that it is concerned mainly with appreciation of human nature. Any piece of undoubted literature will illustrate this; the *Iliad* for example, where the theme is of warlike virtues, the tenderness of women and the sorrows of the unfortunate who bear affliction nobly; where are displayed vicissitudes of fortune and depths of passion by characters who are interesting to us, because they are worthy representatives of humanity.

But the valuations of art and literature are not the same as those of morality. The difference I believe to be this, that in moral conduct we are dealing for purposes of practice with matters of the deepest importance, with property, the protection of life, the maintenance of a good system of family relationships, the state with all its institutions and principles, and the general advancement of civilization. These are fundamental conditions of human welfare. As moral agents we deal with them in a spirit of gravity, if necessary of sternness, which gives a peculiar colouring to our experience. But matters of art, in which for the present purpose I include literature, are not so grave. The main function of the artist is to adorn life and to add to its enjoyment, not to be careful for its necessities. Bad results ensue when men attempt to do moral duties in a dilettante, aesthetic way; or try to use artistic media merely for purposes of preaching.

Confusion of thought may arise from the fact that to some minds literary and artistic matters assume deep importance, and are treated with great gravity. A famous Oxford professor once declared in the common-room that, though he might sometimes have acted contrary to his moral conscience, he had never acted against his grammatical conscience; and a philosophic friend of mine said to me that he would rather have died than written a certain trumpery little book on ethics. It is not amiss that there should be such men; without them we can hardly main-

tain first-class standards of literary craftsman-
ship. But that such a spirit should prevail widely
would not be good for society. It shows a certain
misplacement of emphasis. Not seldom we find
that the agent who has a super-sensitive conscience in regard to art, has a rather dull
conscience in regard to morality.

§ 2. I think that science also is penetrated with
human valuation, though in some of its branches
less evidently than art and literature. By 'science'
I mean all that intellectual sphere in which our
effort is motived by desire to know. And so in
this sense of the word we must include, not
merely the natural sciences, but also history,
philology, philosophy, and all the other matters
of study where the motive is neither aesthetic
nor utilitarian. Now some of these sciences are
manifestly full of human valuation, direct or
indirect. Who, for example, would study philosophy, if he were not sensitive to human good
qualities? This must be true even of the pessimist. The pessimist may believe that the world

is against man and that he can expect no
happiness in it; and he may believe that the
majority of men are evil. But he must, at least,
value man enough to think it worth while to
philosophize about him.

Still more evidently is this true of history.
Can any one study history who is indifferent
to the fortunes of men?

And philology also is human in its interest,
though less directly. A man may study the
language of a people which he does not like,
as may happen to a student of Chinese; or the
dialect of some poor savage race whom he may
never see nor wish to see. But such studies will
usually be made in reference to some wider
interest, and for the sake of understanding other
languages which are spoken by people with
interesting and valuable qualities of their own.

The natural sciences are of all perhaps the
least human, and that is why they can never be
made the staple of education. Those who try
to force them on us by vaunting their utility

convict themselves of misunderstanding utterly the motives which should make men apply themselves to the acquisition of knowledge. The natural sciences are vastly useful; everybody admits that. But what are they useful for? What is utility? Surely, we must answer that things are truly useful only in so far as they help men to live well. No things are useful in so far as they are used by bad men. Things which are useful without any qualification whatever are those which can be made conducive only to a good life. And so the studies which are the best of all are those which can be used for good purposes and not for bad. And these should be the staple of higher education.

But even in those natural sciences in which there seems to be least human nature, there is an element which has indirectly a human interest and is an object of human appreciation. Take chemistry for an example. An able student may enter upon it impelled in the first instance by mere curiosity, which is an instinct that we have in common with animals. Chemistry may seem to stretch before him as a great field inviting exploration, like strange seas and islands before the adventurous voyager. But, when he begins to master the subject, he finds in it a new attraction. The facts of chemistry may cease to be startling from their novelty; but the wonderfulness of their arrangement becomes manifest to him. The laws of chemistry are seen to form a vast and most intricate system, a little of which we have discovered, but most of which is unknown and challenges discovery. Discovery can be made only by constructing hypotheses, and then testing them by experience and observation; in other words, by creating schemes of thought similar in character to the schemes on which things are actually arranged. Now men do not appreciate complexity of system in objects, unless they have learnt to appreciate intellectual power, *i.e.* when they understand the working of powerful minds, and can follow their courses with pleasure. Studied in this way natural science is a high intellectual experience; but it is only advanced students who can enjoy it. In the elementary stages the student finds himself submissively following directions, like a beginner in cookery with a book of recipes.

§ 3. As there is so much that is common to cultural excellence and moral excellence, we are justified in assuming that the same social and political conditions will be favourable to both. No doubt the differences between art and morals are very great; and bad results ensue both for theory and practice, if the differences are overlooked. It is possible for a man to be very unsatisfactory morally but yet an excellent artist, as we know from the example of Benvenuto Cellini. It happens still more often that execrable artists are morally respectable men. Indeed some moral virtues are not easy to reconcile with a consistently high level of artistic work. An artist is usually something of a loafer and procrastinator, because he has to wait on inspiration. It is a fatal mistake to get into those regular habits of production which are so praiseworthy in other walks of life—so many hours daily at the desk, so many pages regularly turned off. From the artistic point of view any sort of irregularity is better than this. The artist assuredly has his own standard of duty; but, as regards his work, it differs much from that of ordinary life. Nevertheless the general enveloping conditions which encourage the two kinds of excellence are much the same. Both for good art and good morality there must be a sufficient supply of wealth; great poverty narrows the outlook of those who suffer from it, so that they can think about nothing but pressing physical necessities; the mass of the people must have dignity and energy, and believe heartily in themselves and in the established system of ideas by which they live; and there must be a leading class with wide appreciations, especially for what is wholesome and basic in human nature.

History shows us that in a civilized nation

cultural interests are sometimes flourishing, sometimes depressed; at one time there are many great intellects at work in this field, and then come years of barrenness. A superficial explanation of this is that a nation has only a fixed amount of energy, like a steam-engine; and if so much goes in one direction, there is so much less available for anything else. The true explanation is rather that the general conditions have changed; in particular, that an unfavourable change has taken place in the leading class.

How the leading class can be maintained at its best will be considered in the next chapter. Here I may say in anticipation that its chief condition of spiritual health is that it should be heartily devoted to the public service, fully in sympathy with the mass of the population, and not dominated by one-sided or sectional appreciations. Then it will be secure from degeneracy and decadence. In the history of nations we find that such are the conjunctures when literature, art and science flourish most;

it is the leading class which is decisively important in all matters of ideas.

In regard to literature there is no recognized antithesis to 'decadent' except 'classical,' which has misleading associations. Writers are non-decadent when they are fully in sympathy with the main stream of national life, and believe whole-heartedly in national ideas. When things are otherwise, decadence sets in. Decadent writers are those who appeal to the taste of a leading class which has lost touch with the mass of the nation, and gets its chief enjoyment from queer experiences. The appreciations of the decadent writer are anti-catholic; he cares only for parts of life, often for the least edifying. Sometimes he really cares for nothing but style. Much of decadent literature is amusing; but more often it is painful and depressing. Its peculiarities are due to grave social evils, which, if not remedied, will lead to general decay and dissolution; as they did in the collapse of the ancient civilization.

CHAPTER V

THE HIGHER INDIVIDUALISM

§ 1. The chief element of virtue, that which I have been discussing so far under the term of human valuation, is altruistic and social. It is outward-looking: it consists in taking interest in persons and things external to oneself; it draws men to co-operate in the general work of society. But there is another element which is not social in this sense. A man shows it when, turning his attention inward, he thinks about himself—his own character, attainments and career—and takes pride in what he is and does. This is what I mean by the Higher Individualism.

This is very different from the Lower Individualism, which is the appetitive selfishness common to all living creatures. Animals are wholly occupied with their physical needs, apart from certain instincts of reproduction and gregarious life. A solitary animal takes no interest in the minds of other creatures. But an individualist in the higher sense must always have other people in view, and take account of their attitude towards himself. His self-interest is possible only in relation to a social system of which he is acutely conscious. Very often men, who are individualistic or selfish in the higher sense, are not selfish in the lower; so long as they get as much honour as they want, they are indifferent to material benefits. While coarsely selfish men are usually content to suffer humiliations, so long as their appetites are satisfied.

Pride is the natural motive which counts for most in the higher individualism. It has of course a social origin, being closely connected with our reactions to approval and disapproval. Co-operating creatures naturally feel sentiments of approval for those of their mates who perform important tasks well, and sentiments of disapproval for those who fail. Dogs seem to be thus endowed; they need it for their hunting.

An intelligent dog takes manifest pleasure in being praised by his master, and is cowed and dejected by scolding. Among men, both leaders and subordinates are sensitive to praise and blame; leaders especially, because they are more self-conscious. But men have something which animals lack, an internal standard of behaviour. An agent can be said to be proud only so far as he has a more or less definite conception or ideal of what he ought to be and do. This ideal he cherishes and feels satisfaction in acting up to it, whether as leader or as subordinate. Thus, he becomes less dependent upon the praise or blame of those immediately around him.

Pride is very conspicuous in the leaders of primitive societies, such as the Homeric. There it is chiefly concerned with matters of war and government. As societies advance, the range of objects expands in relation to which men feel pride, and comes to include everything of intellectual or artistic interest which is prized by civilized men.

§ 2. The typically proud and individualistic man was highly esteemed in the ancient world; and indeed in most of the modern Christian period also, though not with the approval of the official moralists. In recent times there has been a strong reaction against him; and he seems now to be getting less than his deserts. The 'megalopsychic man' of Aristotle has been overwhelmed with ridicule by generations of Oxford students; and it has even been suspected that Aristotle meant him for a caricature. For this reason it seems desirable to study individualism more closely, to estimate its function in a good society and in personal virtue, and to show how it is limited by the master-principle of human value.

It is desirable that everyone should be individualistic or self-interested in the higher sense. However humble a man's work may be, he needs some share of pride. But pride is, most of all, a quality of leaders. Human societies have always needed leaders, and always will. In

advanced societies the work of leadership is so
great that a definite leading class is needed; and
the character of its work requires that it should
have qualities which are different from those of
the rank-and-file.

A born leader must have both the positive
and the negative qualities which give men
authority. He must, above all, desire the praise
or at least the approval of his fellows. In order
to gain this in an eminent degree, he must wish
to be distinguished, that is to rise above the
ordinary level of merit. In the young, who
usually do not know what their needs really are
or what gifts they possess, desire of distinction
may show itself as a vague, restless dissatis-
faction and contempt for their surroundings.
When a leader begins to perform his duties,
one of the most valuable qualities that he can
show is initiative; he must see, earlier than
others, what ought to be done, and take the
lead in getting it done. Initiative is not only a
positive quality; it implies some power of re-

sistance to surrounding mental influences. A man cannot think of new things, if he thinks just like everybody else. A leader is better, indeed, if he is somewhat contra-suggestible, resents being dominated by other minds, and greatly prefers his own ideas and his own methods. And much of the work which a leader has to do is not congenial to a sensitive and sympathetic nature. When Commodore Anson was making his famous voyage round the world, he once more found himself under the cruel necessity of disembarking some of his men upon an unhospitable coast, and leaving them to perish by starvation.

The gifts of command are not entirely compatible with those of sympathy and good nature. A man who desires to rise above the common herd cannot think highly of the common herd. A mind which is contra-suggestible is not fully in harmony with those around. Any one who loves to impose his will on others must give up something of the amiable, benevolent and appreciative qualities of human character. Nor can the dominating and ambitious man pursue a line of personal behaviour such as to bring him into full contact with his fellows. Those who aim at leadership are not inclined to be over-sociable. They adopt an attitude of reserve, lest their friends become too familiar. Sometimes they affect an air of mystery, like Disraeli; for men's imaginations are impressed with the half-unknown. They make it evident that they are not wanting in the sterner qualities of command. They are greatly interested in the development of their own powers and achievements; but less so in the development of others.

The more advanced a society is, the more gifts and accomplishments are needed by its leaders. They need many of the qualities of the student. A spirit of intelligence, a general interest in matters of knowledge should be diffused throughout the whole directing class. A class which is devoted to aims which are antithetic to intellectual excellence—to hunting, shooting and the Turf, or to schemes of military aggression, or to the accumulation of wealth by commerce—will be a stupid and shortsighted class. It will not understand in which direction the true welfare of man lies; it will despise science and disregard the teachings of history.

This intellectual power which is so necessary to our governors is not a mere accumulation of knowledge; it consists also in a strengthening of the imagination. We need imagination more and more, as nations grow bigger and the parts of our social structure become more and more differentiated. No Englishman knows the whole of his country at first-hand, or has had direct contact with more than a very small part of his fellow-citizens. For all the rest he must get help from his imagination. With such hints as can be gained from reading and conversation he must reconstruct mentally lives which are remote from his own. Imagination is indispensable for the governors of great modern states. Without it they are liable to fall into lamentable mistakes; especially in the handling of outlying districts and peoples, who often suffer grievous wrong merely through ignorance of their peculiar needs.

Nor is a directing class satisfactory if it is wanting in artistic culture. No doubt the prime qualification of directing persons is not culture, but the gift of authority. But in order that authority, in civil life at least, may be exercised wisely and without friction, it is necessary that the social director should have fine sympathies and the ability to manage people with tact. Now there is nothing better than artistic culture for improving people in tact. A man who is wanting in these qualities is always wounding people in small matters, even when he treats them fairly in the main. The English show badly in this respect in their intercourse with foreigners. Though recognized as just and honourable, we are generally unpopular from our want of tact; and I think that this is due in some measure to neglect of the fine arts.

All these things increase the distance of the leading class from the common people. The specialization of classes in society is very great, and must increase as higher efficiency is demanded in each several kind of work. Some day it will be seen how dangerous over-specialization is both for the individual and for society; and steps will be taken to counteract it by moving men about from one kind of work to another, so that they do not get estranged from the main interests of mankind. But this is in the future. And whatever steps may be taken, the great number of fine qualities which leaders need will always make them different from those who do the rough work, and carry out orders which they receive from above.

In simple societies leadership and direction are concerned entirely with action; but in advanced societies it is necessary that there should also be men who aspire to leadership in ideas. They have well-recognized functions in science, literature and art, and also in education; but in addition they have a very important social function of which I have already spoken, that of criticizing institutions and of inventing and upholding ideals.

These people are not marked off from the masses by outward circumstance so much as the active leaders are; they have not much need for pomp, and can do their work without putting a physical distance between themselves and the masses. But the mental distance is much greater. The man who leads in ideas must be an intellectual athlete; he must take pleasure in learning and inventing; he will observe with pride the growth of his mental powers and accomplishments. This is very different from the majority of men. Even the upper classes are intellectually soft and lazy for the most part: they hate hard thinking, and avoid difficult subjects of study; the pleasures of the intellectual athlete are unintelligible to them, almost monstrous. Even plainer are the differences of aesthetic taste. In matters of taste the educated man is widely estranged from the half-educated. What *is* it that people like in certain novels, which are 'best-sellers' and yet seem wanting in every element of beauty and truth? How *can* people watch those awful cinema-pictures—some hopelessly silly, some utterly revolting? I suppose it is such thoughts that drive many refined intellects into an anti-democratic attitude; they fear that a flood of vulgarity will submerge everything that is fine and distinguished in life.

For these reasons it is inevitable that in-tellectual leaders should be in large measure out of sympathy with the mass of the population. We may go even beyond this, and maintain that leading minds must have an element of contra-suggestibility which sets them somewhat against environing ideas. This is so even in the sphere of action. An able director must not let himself be subjugated by the traditions of the system which he administers; he must be able to change it, if change is required: and his reaction against the inertia of routine will be strengthened, if he has a native tendency to question established things and to prefer his own way. A social critic needs this quality even more; great docility is incompatible with high critical power. Contra-suggestibility is not a very amiable quality, especially in clever young men who are often bitterly fault-finding without being in the least constructive or helpful. But every nation needs a fair supply of such minds, and nations, in which the born critic is exterminated or muzzled, are sure to sink into stagnation.

§ 3. This then is what I mean by the higher individualism. We must recognize that in it we have a principle of conduct which is different in kind from the social principle which is predominant in our moral experience; we must not reduce all good motives to collectivism: there is more than one principle in our moral life. And yet there is a close relation between the predominant moral principle and this subordinate one. All the interests which raise a man from the lower individualism to the higher are of social origin. The best of our individualist interests, aesthetic sensibilities for example, are mainly partial human valuations. And the aloofness of the individualist is ultimately in the interest of society; because the work of society prospers as a whole, if there are specialists who are devoted to the cultivation of their own gardens.

The danger which besets superior men is that they should overestimate their difference from the masses, ignore their dependence upon the common life, and so become quite estranged from it. In England the danger is serious owing to the economic maladjustments of our present system, and the caste-prejudices which we have inherited from the past. In all our complex modern societies the lower classes inevitably differ from the upper, not only in minor points, such as dress, accent, manners and personal habits, but also in aesthetic taste, ways of thinking and even in matters of moral scruple. These things do put barriers between men; but those who let themselves be alienated from the masses too much are sure to suffer some kind of moral degeneration.

The causes of the class-alienation from which we suffer in this country are mainly economic. A great part of our leading class is parasitic, and performs no service in return for the wealth and honour which it enjoys. This is injurious to social good-will. Whatever philanthropic efforts may be made by individuals, the position of a parasitic class is always odious; it is disliked by the labouring people who maintain it in idleness, and it repays the dislike with scorn. Under unfavourable circumstances a parasitic class may quite lose touch with the ordinary moral standard, which represents the conditions of welfare for ordinary citizens. At any rate it always incurs a danger of sinking into decadence and losing some of the elementary virtues—the men cowardly, and the women bad mothers and wives. Our present English upper-class is so far in touch that its degeneration is not very deep nor universal; its main faults are due to lack of interest in worthy pursuits. Even if the present economic maladjustments were corrected, the danger of class-alienation would not be past, though it would take a different form. What is to be feared in the future is that the upper-class may get too keen and intellectual, and too hard with the hardness of very clever men who are wanting in elementary sympathies and passions; or too aesthetically sensitive, and so disposed to refuse entirely their share in the rough and dirty work which men will always have to perform.

Such anti-collectivist tendencies must be corrected, if we are to reap the full benefit of reforms in our social and political institutions. Institutional reform can do much; but it cannot do everything, and perhaps not even the most important things. The virtue which at the present day seems to me to be most in need of increase is civic devotion. There are some men who have it; men who will work as hard for the state and be as careful and strict in public matters as average men are in matters that redound to their private advantage. But we have not nearly enough of them. The virtue does not pervade society sufficiently. How is it to be increased? We cannot rely much upon precept and exhortation. In Tahiti, it is said, family affection is greatly wanting among the natives. Would it be of much use to try to inculcate it? Instincts which are the basis of morality seem to come into being as they are needed, no one knows how. We must hope that a state of sentiment will grow up such that the very thought of cheating the community, or even of performing public duties slackly, will be abhorrent to the moral sense of the average man.

A great improvement in organization will be made, when superior minds are given more opportunities of interesting themselves in practical affairs than they now enjoy. Young men of good abilities and generous sympathies are attracted irresistibly by high studies—languages, literature, history and philosophy—and strive eagerly to become proficient in them; though later, when their early enthusiasm is satisfied, they are quite willing to go into ordinary harness. But this they cannot do. The prevalent notion among business-men is that a first-rate education disqualifies a man for most kinds of practical service. Business people will not look at such a man as a candidate for employment; his outlook on life and general style is quite alien to theirs. They want some one who is 'pushing,' or one who looks as if he is well able to bully and domineer. Perhaps these are good practical qualifications when the chief motive in business is to make profits for the employer; but less valuable when the chief object is to work efficiently for the public service.

Where political interest and civic devotion are widely diffused among the population, there is a good demos; where those who direct are devoted to the state and are well-instructed, there is a good leading class: these are the circumstances under which a system of democratic control can be brought into effective operation. Because of human frailty no set of men can be trusted with uncontrolled power. The directors of a commonwealth can be kept to their duty by the ordinary methods of influence; by careful selection on appointment, by calling to account, and by praise and blame, rewards and punishments. But the general influence of public opinion is far more potent. When that is sound, our leaders in action and thought can easily be maintained in a right disposition, and never allowed to forget their essential solidarity with the mass of average men.

For EU product safety concerns, contact us at Calle de José Abascal, 56–1°, 28003 Madrid, Spain or eugpsr@cambridge.org.

www.ingramcontent.com/pod-product-compliance
Ingram Content Group UK Ltd.
Pitfield, Milton Keynes, MK11 3LW, UK
UKHW012327130625
459647UK00009B/122